W9-AVX-811

# Flowering Trees of Florida

## Mark K. Stebbins

*Pineapple Press, Inc.*
*Sarasota, Florida*

Inquiries should be addressed to:
Pineapple Press, Inc.
P.O. Box 3889
Sarasota, Florida 34230
www.pineapplepress.com

Library of Congress Cataloging in Publication Data

Stebbins, Mark Knowlden, 1956-
        Flowering trees of Florida / Mark Knowlden Stebbins. - 1st ed.
        p.        cm.
    Includes bibliographical references (p.        ) and index.
    ISBN 1-56164-173-1 (pb : alk. paper)
    1. Flowering trees-Florida.  I. Title.
    SB435.52.F6  S75  1999
    635. 9'7713'09759-dc21
                                                        98-43761
                                                           CIP

First Edition
10 9 8 7 6 5 4 3 2

Design by Mark Stebbins and Osprey Design Systems
Printed in China

**To the late Bob Gilchrist,
who enriched the lives of
all who knew him**

*I'd like to acknowledge the following people for their help and inspiration: Dolores Fugina, Willis Harding, Bill Richardson, Cathy Ryan, and Larry Schokman.*

# Contents

**Note:** Not all trees covered in this book have a common name. When available, the common name is listed in this table of contents.

# Preface

**A**s a boy growing up in northwest New Jersey, I would often observe my father pacing the lawn, watering bucket in hand. He had one of those immaculate lawns with the right plants in the right places. With great anticipation, he looked forward to the bloom cycles of his Forsythia and Rhododendron. To me, these shrubs, with names I could barely pronounce, were just obstacles to the lawn mower and our football games. To my father they were "special" plants that offered an aesthetic gift to those who would pause and take notice.

Eventually my wife and I moved to an acre of land in Florida. Being an avid woodworker, I discovered that many of the world's exotic timbers come from tropical ornamental flowering trees that will grow in the subtropical peninsula of Florida. It was time to see if I had inherited my father's green thumb.

Florida presents some unique challenges and opportunities in the growing of unusual trees. I tried to do some research, but there are few books that adequately cover this topic. I was fortunate to make the acquaintance of nursery owners, horticulturists, and friends in the Tropical Flowering Tree Society of Miami who have been willing to share their knowledge. After deciding to write this book, I spent several years researching and traveling around the state photographing trees.

Of the 74 genera covered in this book, only a few are native to Florida. Most are more spectacular trees from the tropical parts of the world, chosen for their ability to adapt to Florida's subtropical climate—with a little understanding and care. I was tempted to include Plumeria (also called Frangipani), Camellia, and Hibiscus, but these have many hybrids and have been well-covered in other books as well as having their own plant societies (see listings on the World Wide Web).

Today I can understand my father's enthusiasm for these great works of nature. I anxiously anticipate the springtime blooms of my Tabebuia and Jacaranda trees and the fall blossoming of Bauhinia, Chorisia, and Tecoma. I might add that my son wonders why his dad spends so much time looking at trees.

# The Naming of Florida

*Loblolly Bay*

I n the spring of 1513, Juan Ponce de León sailed north from Puerto Rico to search for the island of Bimini and the legendary fountain of youth. On April 2, his ships dropped anchor in what is now the St. Augustine inlet. He claimed the land for Spain and named it *La Florida* after the Easter celebration of flowers, *Pascua Florida*. On April 3, he went ashore.

Many history books neglect to mention this Easter connection and make reference to Florida as the "Land of Flowers." However, central and south Florida have very few native flowering trees, and to travel Florida's many miles of highways is to witness vast tracks of pine forests intermixed with palmetto-laden plains. It wasn't until the early- to mid-twentieth century that some of the world's greatest flowering trees were introduced to the Florida landscape. A nice native Florida tree seen growing today in moist or wet forests in central Florida is *Gordonia lasianthus*, or "Loblolly Bay."

# In Tribute

*A book about the trees of Florida would not be complete without a tribute to two of Florida's outstanding horticulturists.*

# Dr. Edwin A. Menninger

(1896-1995)

In 1922, Ed Menninger moved from New York to Florida to pursue a career as a newspaper editor. In 1928, he purchased the *Stuart Daily News*, which he published for almost 35 years. After watching a travel movie about New Zealand and seeing the magnificent flowering trees in bloom at Christchurch and Plymouth, he inquired at local nurseries, only to find a small selection of flowering plants. Around 1935, he started to make contacts around the world in an effort to obtain tropical tree seeds. He corresponded with hundreds of botanists, explorers, and villagers in order to seek out the world's best ornamental trees.

Menninger estimated that at one time he had over 15,000 seedlings growing in his yard and throughout his neighborhood in Stuart. In the 1940s, he founded and published the *Florida Florist and Nurseryman*. He also served as director of the American Association of Botanical Gardens and Arboretums.

Never formally trained as a botanist, Menninger always took a scientific approach to his hobby, so much so that he received an honorary Doctor of Science degree from Florida State University. Between 1956 and 1964, he wrote six books, including his comprehensive work *Flowering Trees of the World*. I recently spoke to some of the people who knew Ed well. They fondly remember him walking the streets of Stuart, usually with a handful of seeds in his pocket and some good stories to tell about their origin.

# Dr. David Fairchild
(1869-1954)

**A**fter receiving a degree in botany from Kansas State College of Agriculture in 1888 and taking graduate courses at Iowa State and Rutgers, David Fairchild accepted a research assignment in Naples, Italy, representing the Smithsonian Institution. It seemed that Fairchild would go on to pursue the life of a research scholar until he met Barbour Lathrop, a world traveler and explorer who had been to Southeast Asia, a land that held a special interest for Fairchild. Lathrop must have been impressed with the young scientist; a few weeks after meeting him, he offered to send him to Java for research at the famous Buitenzorg Botanical Gardens. Fairchild would study for two years in Germany at Breslau, Berlin, and Bonn to prepare for his trip in 1895.

Fairchild was amazed at the diversity of plants in the Tropics. He quickly abandoned his studies on fungi, molds, and termites and dedicated the rest of his life to the study of fruits, grains, and other commercial plants and how they could be introduced into new environments. He would later comment, "Never to have seen anything but the temperate zone is to have lived on the fringe of the world. Between the tropic of Capricorn and the tropic of Cancer live the majority of all the plant species." He would spend the next eight years traveling the world's tropical regions with Lathrop.

Fairchild returned to Washington, DC, to work for the United States Department of Agriculture (USDA), where he directed the section of Foreign Seed and Plant Introduction from 1906 to 1928. While in Washington, he met Alexander Graham Bell. In 1905, he married Bell's daughter Marian, who would accompany him on future expeditions. While working for the USDA, he was responsible for establishing plant introduction stations in California, Washington

state, North Dakota, Georgia, and Florida. Under his direction, more than 200,000 plant species were introduced in the United States, including multimillion-dollar crop plants such as Russian wheat, Japanese rice, soybeans, Peruvian alfalfa, and Mexican cotton.

At the end of World War I, Fairchild convinced the Secretary of War to donate Chapman Field, an abandoned air-training field in south Miami, to the Department of Agriculture. Fairchild's group transformed 200 acres of the mostly chalky scrubland into a plant introduction station where hundreds of tropical fruits, palms, and ornamental plants would be introduced to North America.

Today, Fairchild is perhaps best recognized by the botanical park that bears his name. The Fairchild Tropical Garden was formally dedicated on March 23, 1938. The 83-acre park is located 12 miles south of Miami on Old Cutler Road and features some of the world's finest collections of palms, flowering trees, and vines from the Tropics—a suitable tribute to one of America's best-known agricultural explorers.

# Botanical Names

**W**hen we don't know the name of a tree, we often resort to using phrases such as "the tree with the yellow, bell-shaped flowers." We may even use a nickname such as "Golden Trumpet Tree." While this method may suffice for casual conversation, it does not bode well for the positive identification of trees.

During the 1500s, when the list of known plants grew from a thousand to tens of thousands, botanists were developing new methods to classify plants. Many systems emerged, but it wasn't until the mid 1700s that a universally accepted method took hold. That system, developed by the distinguished Swedish botanist Carl Linnaeus, groups plants with similar characteristics into a genus. Unique plants (plants that can reproduce among themselves) were given a species name. Different plants can share the same species name; however, the combination of genus and species names defines a unique plant. During the time of Linnaeus, Latin was the common language of European scientists and was the natural choice for naming plants under this new system.

We are fortunate that this system has maintained its universal acceptance to this day. For example, the "Royal Poinciana," as we know it in Florida, goes by many names in different parts of the world; however, its botanical name, *Delonix regia*, is recognized whether you are in China, Egypt, or South Africa. For the home gardener, learning the botanical names of trees has several advantages: Seed catalogs use botanical names; botanical gardens use them to label plants; and botanical names will help you to recognize common features of a genus, which helps in identification.

Unfortunately, these names are not easy to remember or pronounce. Latin is no longer the dominant language of science, and the pronunciation of botanical names is heavily influenced by one's native tongue (although there are those who still promote the use of classical Latin).

I hope that the pronunciation guides provided in this book will encourage you to use botanical names. This interpretation is strongly biased towards English with a few exceptions. The "c" in *grandiceps* and *speciosa* is pronounced with an "s" sound instead of the Latin "k" sound. A terminal vowel is "strong" or "hard." For example, the terminal "i" in *grandidieri* and *boissieri* is pronounced as in "high." Exceptions are *crista-galli*, which uses the Latin "ee" sound, and *Erythrina* and *Tibouchina*, which terminate with the Latin "ee-na."

A pronunciation is offered for each Latin name, using a spelling for each syllable that provides an easily recognized English pronunciation. The accented syllable appears in CAPS.

# Albizia

(al-BIZ-ee-a)
FABACEAE
**Silk Tree**

This genus was named by Antonio Duranzzini in 1772 after the Italian noble-man Filippo degli Albizzi, who started cultivating the Silk Tree in the mid-1700s.

### *Albizia julibrissin*
(yoo-lee-BRIS-in)
The Silk Tree or Mimosa is a small deciduous tree that can reach a height of 30 feet. It has a broad crown with fine foliage and flowers tinged red or pink. Its natural habitat ranges from Iran through northern India, Nepal, China, and Japan. Its fernlike, bipinnate leaves are comprised of small (less than one half inch), oblong leaflets that close at night. (See leaf comparison photos on page 133.) Flowers are a ball-like array of stamens. Seed pods are long, flat, and tan. Bloom occurs in late spring or early summer, when this tree puts on a nice display of color. Another member of the *Albizia* genus found in Florida is *Albizia lebbeck*. With leaflets up to

*Albizia julibrissin*
Silk Tree

one and a half inches long, the foliage is not as finely textured. The flowers are off-white or tan. Although not as ornamental, this tree contains wood that looks much like Eastern Black Walnut (*Juglans nigra*).

### Cultivation

The Silk Tree grows fast from seed. Some training is required in its early youth to shape the tree and trim up low branches. It will adapt to a variety of soil types, and once established, it is drought-tolerant. It will keep its leaves longer and look greener if provided a steady source of water. It is not recommended for beachside planting. The Silk Tree sheds flowers in the summer and leaflets and seed pods in the fall, so some extra maintenance is required. Planting at the base of a hill or under a second-story window may provide extra visibility to the bloom, since the flowers are produced on top of the canopy. The Silk Tree is hardy in all parts of Florida; a variety called "Rosea" is grown as far north as Maryland. Wilt disease is a concern in the southern states, but the varieties "Charlotte" and "Tryon" are resistant.

*Albizia julibrissin*
Silk Tree

# Bauhinia

(bow-HIN-ee-a)
CAESALPINIACEAE
**Orchid Trees**

The trees belonging to the genus *Bauhinia* comprise one of the most widely cultivated tropical ornamental groups. The genus was named by Carl Linnaeus in honor of the sixteenth-century botanists John and Casper Bauhin. The Bauhin brothers were originally trained as physicians, but like many doctors of their time, they were also trained in botany, and their publications in this field were used for many years.

*Bauhinia* is a diverse genus comprised of over 200 species of vines, shrubs, and small- to medium-size trees found throughout the world's tropical regions. *Bauhinia* is most often recognized by its bifid (dual-lobed) leaf form. Several medium-size species established in the United States can reach a height of 25 to 30 feet. They are native to India, China, and Southeast Asia, and in many parts of the world are known as "orchid" trees for their showy displays of orchidlike flowers.

*Bauhinia blakeana*
Hong Kong Orchid Tree

*Bauhinia variegata "Candida"*
Mountain Ebony

*Bauhinia blakeana*
(blake-ee-AH-na)
The Hong Kong Orchid Tree blooms profusely from fall through spring and has a short deciduous period (it is nearly evergreen in tropical regions). The flowers are rose-violet and keep their color. It is considered to be a hybrid between *Bauhinia variegata* and *Bauhinia purpurea* and is sterile (no seed pods). This tree is often referred to as one of the outstanding flowering trees of the world. In the July 1954 issue of the *National Horticultural Magazine*, Bruce Ledin wrote, "It is believed to have been discovered by monks of the Roman Cathedral of Canton who found a single tree growing near the ruins of a house along the seashore near Canton. Cuttings were taken and successfully rooted. Later, it was planted in the Hong Kong Botanical Garden. *Bauhinia blakeana* was named in 1908 for Sir Henry Blake, the governor of Hong Kong and supporter of the Hong Kong Botanical Garden. In 1958, Kyoshi Ichimura, a Japanese industrialist, donated 300 of the trees to the city of Miami."

Orchid trees have fragrant flowers that attract butterflies and hummingbirds. A perfumed aroma was noticeable in the air as I stood underneath the large Hong Kong Orchid Tree shown in the photo below.

*Bauhinia blakeana*
Hong Kong Orchid Tree

*Bauhinia purpurea*
(pur-PEWR-ee-a)
This orchid tree blooms in the fall. The flowers have three stamens and are about five inches wide. The branches are long and slender. A common name for *Bauhinia purpurea* is Fall Orchid Tree. Its flower color varies from light pink to red or purple. This variation can be a source of confusion in the identification of *Bauhinia purpurea*; however, the color will come true from seed. The near-white specimen with reddish-brown veining, shown on page 18, was photographed at the Singapore Botanic Gardens. There are no pure white versions of this species.

*Bauhinia purpurea*
Fall Orchid Tree

*Bauhinia purpurea*
Fall Orchid Tree

*Bauhinia purpurea*
Fall Orchid Tree

*Bauhinia variegata*
(vair-ee-a-GAH-ta)
This tree blooms in late winter and spring. Unlike *Bauhinia purpurea,* which has tree-to-tree color variation, *Bauhinia variegata* color variation appears within its flower. The flower contains shades of purple from very light to very dark on the primary petal. The flower size is slightly smaller (about four inches) with five stamens; the petals are broader than *Bauhinia purpurea* and overlap. *Bauhinia variegata* has a white cultivar called *Bauhinia variegata* "Alba" or "Candida." The primary petal on these flowers can have yellow or green veining or can be completely white. As with *Bauhinia purpurea,* flowering is followed by six- to eight-inch, flat, narrow seed pods. The reddish-brown wood from this tree is hard and heavy with an attractive grain. This explains its common name, Mountain Ebony.

*Bauhinia variegata*
Mountain Ebony

*Bauhinia variegata*
Mountain Ebony

*Bauhinia variegata "Candida"*
Mountain Ebony

*Bauhinia monandra*
(moh-NAN-dra)
Sometimes called the Pink Orchid Tree, this beautiful ornamental comes from Burma. Large flowers are produced from May through November. It is quite sensitive to cold weather; several degrees above freezing can cause damage. The color varies from creamy-white to light pink. The top petal has spattered areas of pink or red, and the colors become more uniform as the flower ages. The flower has only one stamen.

*Bauhinia monandra*
Pink Orchid Tree

*Bauhinia monandra*
Pink Orchid Tree

There are several smaller, less common species of *Bauhinia* that have been introduced into the United States. These trees are often multistem or shrub-shaped but are easily trained as single trunk specimens that can grow to 10 to 15 feet.

### *Bauhinia aculeata*
(a-kew-lee-AH-ta)

This summer bloomer has divided leaves (one-fourth cleft) with pointed lobes. The three- to four-inch white flowers have five spaced petals—which are lanceolate, long, and narrowing at the base—and ten stamens. This tree originated in the lesser Antilles, Central America, and northern South America. The branches are armed with curved thorns, with two at each node. My good friend and *Bauhinia* collector, Bob Gilchrist, points out that there are two varieties of this species: One has two- to three-inch, dull white flowers; another grows to 20 feet with large, pure white, "showy" flowers and is sometimes given the name *Bauhinia mollicella*.

*Bauhinia aculeata*
Aculeata

### Bauhinia acuminata
(a-kew-min-AH-ta)

The Dwarf White Bauhinia is native to areas from India to Malaysia. It was introduced in Florida sometime before 1900. Showy white flowers are produced on racemes throughout the summer. Its petals are broad and overlap, and it has ten stamens.

*Bauhinia acuminata*
Dwarf White Bauhinia

*Bauhinia galpinii*
African Red Bauhinia

*Bauhinia galpinii*
(GAL-pin-ee-eye)
In the wild, this species is a woody vine that grows to ten feet and forms a rounded mass similar to Bougainvillea. Like Bougainvillea, it can be trained into a tree form. This attractive plant from Southern Africa has small (one- to two-inch), hoof-shaped, rounded leaves and abundant brick-red flowers throughout summer and into fall. There are also less common orange and yellow cultivars. It can be grown in zone 9 but rarely sets seed outside of zone 10. Common names are Nasturtium Bauhinia (referring to the flowers of the genus) and African Red Bauhinia. Seeds are often sold under the name *Bauhinia punctata*.

*Bauhinia galpinii*
African Red Bauhinia

*Bauhinia divaricata*
(die-vair-i-KAH-ta)
Considered a large shrub, this species is native to Mexico, Central America, and the Greater Antilles. It has small (one- to two-inch) flowers, with white petals that sometimes turn pink with age, and one stamen. The leaves have pointed lobes and are cleft to about one third; however, the size and shape can vary. They have been grown in some areas of zone 8 and may be one of the more cold-hardy species of *Bauhinia*. I recently saw a specimen grown from a cutting. It was covered with blooms and made a handsome bonsai. In the Caribbean, this tree is called Pata de Vaca.

*Bauhinia divaricata*
Pata de Vaca

*Bauhinia tomentosa*
(toh-men-TOH-sa)
Known as Yellow Bell Bauhinia, this species has flowers with overlapping petals that remain bell-shaped and never fully open. The primary petal is usually marked with a dark brown spot near the base, although sometimes it's pure yellow. This widely cultivated species from tropical Asia and Africa can vary in leaf shape and growth pattern. Some plants have leaves divided two thirds of the length and an upright growth habit. Other specimens have leaves almost fully divided and have a sprawling shrub shape. It has been suggested that the latter variety is from Africa.

*Bauhinia tomentosa*
Yellow Bell Bauhinia

### Bauhinia grandidieri
(gran-di-DEE-rye)
A native of Madagascar, this species grows to about 12 feet. Small leaves are fully divided. Flowers are about one inch across and are light mauve. It was named in honor of plant explorer Alfred Grandidier (1836-1921).

*Bauhinia grandidieri*
Bauhinia

*Bauhinia rufescens*
Menninger's Bauhinia

*Bauhinia rufescens*
(ROOF-a-senz)

This small African tree was introduced by Dr. Edwin Menninger during the 1940s. It has small, highly divided leaves about one-half inch across. The flowers are white or pale yellow with ten stamens and are slightly larger than the leaves. They are produced on short racemes several times a year. The fruits are coiled pods. Branches tend to grow in planes similar to *Bauhinia grandidieri*. The tree, which can grow to 15 feet tall, is not showy in bloom but may have greater ornamental appeal if trained as a bonsai.

*Bauhinia semla*
(SEM-la)

Native to Northern India and Nepal, this tree can reach over 20 feet tall with nearly round leaves notched slightly at the apex. The flowers measure about one inch across and are white or light cream with dark, red-purple spots. Numerous flowers are loosely spaced on upright panicles during the fall months, giving the tree a "frosted" look. Although the tree was introduced into Florida by the USDA in 1934 under the name *Bauhinia roxburghiana*, it is today a rare find. So far, the saplings I'm growing show good tolerance to near-freezing temperatures. Seeds are sometimes sold under the name *Bauhinia retusa*.

### Cultivation

Orchid trees have few pests and are easy to grow. The main consideration is keeping them fed with micronutrients and making sure the soil is acidic (pH range of 5.5-7.0). Leaf burn can be a problem, especially toward the end of the year before new growth comes in.

Prune lightly after bloom but only to shape the tree. *Bauhinia* likes full sun but will tolerate some shade. Propagate from cuttings, layering, or seed (except for *Bauhinia blakeana*, which does not produce seed).

The larger trees are most often classified as zone 10; however, many fine specimens can be found in zone 9. *Bauhinia variegata* and *Bauhinia galpinii* have been known to survive temperatures down to 20° F. Prune damaged areas in the spring. Mature trees usually make a good recovery.

***Bauhinia semla***
North Indian Bauhina

# Bombax

(BOM-baks)
BOMBACACEAE
**Red Silk Cotton, Shaving Brush Tree**

The name *Bombax* originates from the Greek word for silk, *bombyx,* and refers to the silk- or cottonlike fibers that fill the seed pods. The three species covered here are noted for their ornamental flowers and potentially large dimensions.

*Bombax ceiba*
(SAY-ba)
This large tree, also known as *Bombax malabaricum*, comes from India, Burma, and Central America. It's the national tree of Guatemala and was considered sacred by Mayan Indians. Introduced into Florida in the late 1800s, *Bombax* trees can be found growing in the lower half of the state, where some have become tourist attractions. Some trees in Florida are over 140 feet tall and over 8 feet in diameter at the base. They drop their leaves in the winter and bloom

*Bombax ceiba*
Red Silk Cotton

*Bombax ceiba*
Red Silk Cotton

before putting out new foliage. The large (six-inch), crimson-red flowers cluster at the branch tips and have many stamens tipped with purple anthers. The tree, shown on page 31, can be found at Cypress Gardens in Winter Haven, Florida. It leans over the French Garden and shades the entire area during the summer.

The large seed pods, produced after bloom, eventually break open and disperse clumps of cottonlike fibers with embedded seeds. In India, the soft fibers are collected and are used to stuff pillows. Many Floridians know this tree by the name Kapok. In the Tropics, however, Kapok is used to describe a related tree, *Ceiba pentandra,* that is not considered ornamental. Most American botanists prefer to use the name Red Silk Cotton. The palmately compound leaves are grayish green and vary from five to nine leaflets.

## *Pseudobombax ellipticum*
(e-LIP-ti-kum )

This unusual tree is very different from *Bombax ceiba*, although it was once listed under the genus *Bombax*. Native to Central America, it is often referred to as the Shaving Brush Tree. It usually stays under 30 feet tall on Florida lawns, but can grow as tall as the specimen at Fairchild Tropical Garden in Miami (see photo on next page). It has a smooth, green trunk and blooms in the spring when bare of leaves. These trees produce a flower with a cluster of long stamens. The flower is unique and is sure to capture the attention of passersby. Consisting of five purple-brown petals fused together in a cigar shape, it bursts open during the night to reveal a cluster of silky pink stamens, each tipped with a gold anther. A variation of this tree produces white sta-

*Pseudobombax ellipticum*
Shaving Brush Tree

*Pseudobombax  ellipticum*
Shaving Brush Tree

*Pseudobombax  ellipticum*
Shaving Brush Tree

mens. By mid to late afternoon, the flowers drop to the ground. Flowering continues for two to four weeks followed by new foliage. The palmate leaves consist of five leaflets that are red when young, becoming green and large when mature. *Pseudobombax ellipticum* is some-times confused with a related species, also grown in Florida, called Water Chestnut (genus *Pachira)*. These trees flower when the leaves are on the tree, which sometimes hide the flowers, and yield a seed pod that contains chestnut-sized seeds and no "cotton."

*Pseudobombax ellipticum (new leaves)*
Shaving Brush Tree

*Pachira aquatica*
Water Chestnut

*Bombax rhodognaphalon*
(roh-do-NAF-a-lon)
While photographing *Chorisias* at the Willis Harding Flowering Tree Park in Miami Lakes, my attention was drawn to a tree with attractive white flowers. At first glance, it looked like *Chorisia insignis*, but close inspection revealed smooth, fleshy petals similar to those of *Bombax ceiba*. The tree; *Bombax rhodognaphalon,* is rarely found in cultivation. Sometimes called *Rhodognaphalon brevicuspe*, it is native to the forests of West Africa from Sierra Leone to Gabon. It blooms in the fall and continues for several months. Blooms are solitary or in small groups.

The Willis Harding Park, located a few miles north of the Miami International Airport at NW 188TH and NW 62ND Streets, has a wide variety of trees in the Bombacaceae family such as *Chorisia, Bombax, Ceiba, Pachira,* and *Rhodognaphalon.*

## Cultivation

Red Silk Cotton needs a warm and humid environment to prosper. The seeds germinate readily and grow rapidly. Some saplings have spikes (similar to *Chorisia*); some don't. The thorns are shed as the tree matures. Enriched, sandy soil is best, and remember to give them a lot of room!

Although the Shaving Brush Tree can produce a Kapok floss, it does not produce seed in Florida. Most trees are propagated by air layering or cuttings. Soil requirements are similar to Red Silk Cotton, except that Shaving Brush adapts better to drought. Potted plants sometimes produce a swollen base. Both trees are sensitive to frost, but mature Red Silk Cotton trees have been known to survive overnight temperatures to the low 20s.

Bombax trees are sensitive to salt and should be planted away from the beach.

*Bombax rhodognaphalon*
Rhodognaphalon

# Brownea

(BROWN-ee-a)
CAESALPINIACEAE
**Scarlet Flame Bean, Rose of Venezuela**

In *Flowering Trees of the Caribbean*, the authors detailed the trials and tribulations of transplanting tropical plants from South America to England during the early 1800s. The plants were kept in special casks that were fastened to the ships' decks. During good weather, they were brought out on the top deck and frequently given sponge baths to remove salt spray. Many plants perished, but one that survived, to the delight of European greenhouse operators, was *Brownea*. The genus was named after Dr. Patrick Browne, a noted naturalist from Ireland who lived in Jamaica from 1746 to 1755. Browne later went on to become the curator of the Oxford Botanical Garden, where he described hundreds of Jamaican species. There are about 25 species of *Brownea*, all coming from the tropical regions of Venezuela and neighboring countries.

*Brownea capitella*
Scarlet Flame Bean

*Brownea capitella*
(ka-pi-TELL-a)
The Scarlet Flame Bean is a small evergreen tree with weeping foliage. The brightly colored flowers, up to one foot across, have long, exerted stamens—truly outstanding. This species is also considered to be a variation of *Brownea coccinea.*

*Brownea grandiceps*
(GRAND-i-seps)
The Rose of Venezuela is described in Hortus III as a "handsome tree to 60 ft." This prolific bloomer bears its flowers in tight clusters up to nine inches across at the ends of branches. (Note: Some *Brownea* species bear flowers along the branches. The flower in the photo was leaning over a branch.) *Brownea ariza* is sometimes classified as a separate species, but it has also been listed as a synonym for *Brownea grandiceps.*

### Cultivation

*Brownea* is propagated from seed or cuttings. The seed is as rare as the trees themselves. In Florida, you can see them at Fairchild Tropical Garden in Miami. *Brownea* grows in semi-shaded or shaded areas, prefers enriched soil with plenty of heat and moisture, and will bloom in a greenhouse.

*Brownea grandiceps*
Rose of Venezuela

# Bulnesia

(bul-NEE-see-a)
Zygophyllaceae
**Vera Wood**

While visiting a coastal city in Venezuela, Dr. David Fairchild noticed a small tree in a village courtyard. At a distance he thought it was a *Cassia* because of its fine pinnate leaflets and yellow flowers. On closer inspection, he identified it as *Bulnesia*. This genus of about nine species of shrubs and trees was named by Claude Gay (1800-1873). Fairchild was the first to introduce *Bulnesia* to the United States; the trees he brought can still be seen at the Fairchild Tropical Garden in Miami.

### *Bulnesia arborea*
(ar-BOR-ee-a)

This evergreen tree grows to 40 feet, although some have been reported to reach 100 feet. Native to Columbia and Venezuela, it is common in the dry foothills between Porto Cabello and Lake Maracaibo. A nicely shaped tree with attractive pinnate leaflets, it produces buttery yellow blooms three times a year from spring to fall.

Double flowers are produced at branch tips. As a member of the Zygophyllaceae family, it is related to Lignum Vitae (*Guaiacum*); its lumber has many of the same hard and heavy characteristics. In the timber trade, its called Vera Wood or Maracaibo Lignum Vitae. A related species, *Bulnesia retama,* produces retamo wax used in shoe polish.

*Bulnesia arborea*
Vera Wood

### Cultivation

Plant *Bulnesia* in a sunny location. It adapts to a wide variety of soils, and once established it is drought-tolerant. Propagate from seed or air layering. Seed may take a month or more to germinate. The grow rate is slow to moderate. Several nurseries in the Miami area now offer *Bulnesia* *arborea*. The temperature tolerance of *Bulnesia* is unknown. The tree I planted in my central Florida lawn encountered several light frosts this past winter and retained its leaves and nice appearance. However, since it is related to Lignum Vitae, it would probably suffer in a freeze.

*Bulnesia arborea*
Vera Wood

# Caesalpinia

(says-al-PEE-nee-a)
CAESALPINIACEAE
**Dwarf Poinciana, Brazilian Ironwood, Mexican Poinciana**

This genus of up to 60 mostly tropical and subtropical small trees is concentrated in Central and South America and the Caribbean. Some are cultivated as ornamentals; others are noted for producing exotic lumber. *Caesalpinia* is named after the Italian physician-botanist Andrea Caesalpino (1519-1603).

*Caesalpinia pulcherrima*
(pul-CARE-ri-ma)
This species is the most common *Caesalpinia* grown in Florida. In the Caribbean, it's called Pride of Barbados and grows to 20 feet. In Florida, where it is called Dwarf Poinciana, it is usually bushy and rarely exceeds 10 feet. Large clusters of showy flowers are displayed above the foliage several times from spring through fall. *Caesalpinia pulcherrima* has rose-like thorns and delicate, lacy foliage, as do most members of *Caesalpinia*. Color combinations include red-yellow, pink-cream, and solid yellow. The long "whisker" stamens tipped with golden anthers draw attention to the beautiful flower.

*Caesalpinia pulcherrima*
Dwarf Poinciana

*Caesalpinia pulcherrima*
Dwarf Poinciana

*Caesalpinia pulcherrima*
Dwarf Poinciana

## Caesalpinia ferrea
(FAIR-ee-a)

This Brazilian tree grows to 30 feet with clusters of golden flowers during the summer. Other notable features include a smooth, mottled bark and hard, dense wood. Common names are Brazilian Ironwood and Leopard Bark. The wood is dark brown with thin black streaks. It reminds me of the classic Brazilian rosewoods of the genus *Dalbergia*. Although rare in Florida, a mature *Caesalpinia ferrea* can be seen at Marie Selby Botanical Gardens in Sarasota. A close relative to *Caesalpinia ferrea* is the famous *Caesalpinia echinata*. Although lacking attractive flowers, the red dye produced from the wood was an important Brazilian export. The wood is called Brazil Wood or Pernambuco, and for professional violinists, there is no substitute for making bows.

*Caesalpinia ferrea*
Brazilian Ironwood, Leopard Bark

*Caesalpinia vesicaria*
(ves-i-CARE-ee-a)
This attractive tree from Central America and the Antilles blooms in the fall or early winter. Many yellow flowers are crowded on upright panicles and make a nice contrast against the deep green, glossy foliage. This small evergreen tree or large shrub is particularly suited for south Florida and warm coastal regions, as it tolerates drought and limestone soils.

*Caesalpinia vesicaria*
Vesicaria

*Caesalpinia mexicana*
(meks-i-KAH-na)
As the name implies, this tree comes from Mexico, but it is also native to Texas. One of the more cold-hardy species, it can be grown throughout zone 9 and in some areas of zone 8. Fast growing from seed, it blooms when young. Although it never covers its canopy with bloom, it produces spikes of yellow flowers throughout the year. It has no thorns and grows to 20 feet.

*Caesalpinia mexicana*
Mexican Poinciana

### Cultivation

Propagate *Caesalpinia* from seed. Use the nick-and-soak method. Provide an ample supply of water for best flowering; however, the soil should allow for good drainage. *Caesalpinia pulcherrima* can be lightly pruned after bloom to stimulate additional bloom or sharply pruned in late winter to shape the tree. *Caesalpinia pulcherrima* is evergreen in South Florida and deciduous in Central Florida. It will take some frost. For areas that encounter frequent frost, growing *Caesalpinia* in tubs is a good option, because it does not have aggressive roots.

*Caesalpinia mexicana*
Mexican Poinciana

# Cassia

(KAS-ee-a)
CAESALPINIACEAE
**Shower Trees, Cassia**

This is a large genus of more than 500 species that range from shrubs to trees native to the Tropics as well as to dry regions. (Some authorities have moved several species to the genus *Senna*.) Most *Cassias* produce yellow flowers with five petals.

*Cassia fistula*
Golden Shower

*Cassia fistula*
(fis-TEW-la)
The most famous of all *Cassias*, this tree has been cultivated in India for more than 2,000 years. The native range is difficult to determine, as *Cassia fistula* has been widely cultivated for so many years. India and Egypt are the most probable regions. The Egyptians valued the seed pods for medicinal purposes, and it is be- lieved that the "Rajataru," or "king of trees," in the Hindu religion is *Cassia fistula*. Spanish conquistadors introduced it to the West Indies and South America. Floridians and Hawaiians call it Golden Shower.

*Cassia fistula*'s brilliant yellow flowers hang down in drooping sprays. It has one of the largest leaves of the *Cassia* genus (about six inches

*Cassia fistula*
Golden Shower

long) arranged in four to eight pairs. In Florida, the tree blooms during the spring and summer after a brief deciduous period. It has a medium-to-fast growth rate depending on the soil and water. These conditions will also produce variations in leaf color, from light green to dark green to leaves with a copper cast. The seed pods are one to two feet in length and are cylindrical. The seeds are suspended in a sticky pulp that smells like licorice. In some parts of the world, the pulp is used as a laxative, and the blossoms are eaten and are considered a delicacy. The hard, red heartwood is a high-priced cabinet lumber; its durability also makes it suitable for outdoor use.

*Cassia javanica*
Apple Blossom Cassia

*Cassia javanica*
(ja-VAH-ni-ka)
This tree is one of several pink flowering species prized for delicate, pink, variegated blossoms that remind Northerners of apple blossoms. The tree is often referred to as the Apple Blossom Cassia. Native to Southeast Asia, it's typically a small tree, sometimes growing to 35 feet with spreading branches. The leaves are two to four inches long and appear in five to twelve pairs. Flowers are produced along the extreme branches during the summer months starting in June. Some-times spikes are found on mature branches and on the trunk. The trees that come from areas north of Malaysia have a green calyx (instead of brown) and are sometimes listed under the species *nodosa*, although many authorities now consider them variations of the same species. One reference lists the northern variety as *javanica* var. *indochinensis* (Gagnepain). Cross breeding of *fistula* and *javanica* has produced multicolored varieties called Rainbow Shower that have shades of yellow, white, and pink.

*Cassia javanica*
Apple Blossom Cassia

### Cassia afrofistula
(af-ro-fis-TEW-la)

This evergreen tree from East Africa has flowers arranged on vertical spikes. They can be seen at the Marie Selby Botanical Gardens in Sarasota. They can flower several times a year and can withstand several degrees of frost.

*Cassia afrofistula*
East African Cassia

*Cassia afrofistula*
East African Cassia

*Cassia leptophylla*
(LEP-toh-fil-a)
This beautiful tree comes from Brazil. Leaves are in eight to twelve ovate-lanceolate pairs. The outstanding specimen shown in the photograph below, grows at the Walt Disney Epcot resort in Orlando. This nearly evergreen tree deserves wider use due to its attractive bloom and shapely appearance.

*Cassia leptophylla*
Golden Medallion Tree

*Cassia bicapsularis*
(bye-kap-sew-LAIR-is)
This small *Cassia* is native to tropical America. It has obovate leaves of only three to five pairs. In its natural state, it will grow up to 12 feet high as a multistem upright shrub, but judicious pruning can shape it into a small tree, perfect in an entryway or as a potted patio specimen. *Cassia bicapsularis* is a winter bloomer that often puts on an intense display around the holiday season. Common names are Winter Cassia and Christmas Cassia. It sometimes is referred to as *Cassia candolleana.*

*Cassia bicapsularis*
Winter Cassia

### Cultivation

These trees prefer full sun and sandy-loam, well-drained soil. Pruning is recommended to improve shape and bloom. *Cassia* seeds are designed to go in the ground for a long time and can remain viable for months. To speed up germination, pour boiling water over them and let soak overnight before planting. Grafting mature *Cassia fistula* or *Cassia javanica* scions onto young root stock will produce blooms on young specimens; from seed, this can take from three to five years. *Cassia javanica* seedlings should be kept at temperatures above 50° F. At lower temperatures, they are susceptible to fungus and insect attack. Both *Cassia fistula* and *Cassia javanica* contain very hard wood that is bright yellow when freshly cut but turns darker shades of brown with age.

*Cassia bicapsularis*
Winter Cassia

# Chorisia

(koh-RIS-ee-a)
BOMBACACEAE
**Silk Floss Tree**

This genus of perhaps three to five species is known in Florida as the Silk Floss Tree. It was named after the artist L. L. Choris, who accompanied Otto Van Kotzebue on South American expeditions. Like other members of the Bombacaceae family, these trees produce a seed pod filled with silklike "cotton" in which the seeds are embedded. *Chorisia* is known for its ornamental flowers and for the ominous thorns that cover its trunk and branches.

### *Chorisia speciosa*

(spee-see-OH-sa)
This species is the most cultivated of the *Chorisia* genus, and can put on an impressive floral display around October and November, when the leaves drop. The curious diversity of *Chorisia speciosa* flower coloration from tree to tree is not replicated from seed. Dr. Edwin Menninger sought the help of the scientific community to help further classify this species but ended up doing a lot of

*Chorisia speciosa*
Silk Floss Tree

*Chorisia speciosa*
Silk Floss Tree

research on his own. Flowers are either pink, rose, or violet at the outer half of the petal. The inner portion can be creamy-white or yellow with dark streaks that radiate from the center. The staminal column is usually fused together along its entire length but is sometimes found with the filaments partially or completely separated. The name "Majestic Beauty" is used to describe a variety with rose-violet on the outer portion of the petal and creamy-white with dark brown streaks on the inner portion. Leaves are palmately compound with five to seven leaflets. *Chorisia speciosa* and *Bombax ceiba* saplings look very similar when not in bloom. The color of the bark distinguishes them: *Chorisia* is predominately green, while *Bombax* is predominately brown.

*Chorisia speciosa*
Silk Floss Tree

*Chorisia insignis*
(in-SIG-nis)
Originating from Peru, this species is grown in California but is rarely seen in Florida. The flowers, less variegated than those of *Chorisia speciosa,* are typically either a creamy-white or golden-yellow.

### Cultivation

*Chorisia* is grown from seed. It's sometimes offered in nurseries, but I believe people who are not familiar with the tree are initially intimidated by the thorns. I recently planted one in my yard after removing the thorns at the base (they pop off readily when tapped on the side with a hammer). Saplings are frost-sensitive, but mature trees are quite cold-tolerant. A number of Silk Floss Trees in central Florida survived the "big freeze" of 1989, when temperatures plummeted to 20° F and below.

*Chorisia speciosa* has been planted at the airport in Miami, at the Disney theme parks in Orlando, and at many botanical gardens in between. They are not particular about soil type. Choose a sunny location with room to spare. *Chorisia* will grow up to 60 feet if crowded, but given room and perhaps some pruning, it will develop a full shape and provide bloom low to the ground. These trees can fill the autumn sky with shades of pink.

*Chorisia insignis*
Silk Floss Tree

# Cochlospermum

(kok-loh-SPER-mum)
COCHLOSPERMACEAE
**Buttercup Tree**

A genus of yellow flowering shrubs and small trees native to the Tropics, *Cochlospermum* was named by the German botanist Carl Kunth in 1822. The name comes from the Greek words *kochlos,* meaning "shellfish," and *sperma,* meaning "seed," referring to the seed's spiral shape, somewhat like a snail's shell. In Florida, a tree in this genus is called Buttercup Tree or Yellow Silk Cotton.

### *Cochlospermum vitifolium*

(vie-ti-FO-lee-um )
This species is native to the tropical regions of the Americas, from Mexico through Central America and the West Indies. The large ornamental flowers bloom on branch tips in the spring when the trees are nearly bare of leaves. Flowers are a brilliant yellow and are about four to five inches across with five petals. A "double" variety produces numerous petals and resembles a rose or camellia. Orange stamens, about half the length of a petal, are clustered in the center of each flower. The growth rate is slow to moderate; trees can grow up to 40 feet tall but usually reach only 20 feet on Florida lawns. Long, spreading branches grow upwards to form a flat or slightly rounded crown. Leaves are six to twelve inches across and have five lobes, each lobe tapering to a point. The fruit is a three- to four-inch-long capsule filled with cottonlike fibers in which the seeds are embedded. Natives use the cotton for stuffing pillows and mattresses. The German word for cotton is *baumwolle,* or "tree-wool," which makes you wonder if the word was influenced more by several tropical trees mentioned in this book than by the cotton-producing shrub of the genus *Gossypium.*

### Cultivation

*Cochlospermum* is propagated by seed or cuttings. Cuttings have a good success rate, and this is the preferred method for the "double" variety, which is sterile. These trees will grow in a wide variety of soils as long as they have good drainage. They adapt well to nutrient-poor, rocky soils in which some of the best specimens can be found growing in the wild. Once established, they require little maintenance.

*Cochlospermum vitifolium*
Buttercup Tree

# Cordia

(KOR-dee-a)
BORAGINACEAE
**Geiger Tree, Texas Wild Olive**

*Cordia* is a large genus of tropical trees, several of which are native to the United States. The genus is named for the German botanist Valerius Cordus (1515–1544). Several species are known as outstanding ornamentals, and others as producers of high grade lumber.

### *Cordia sebestena*

(seb-ah-STEN-a)
Known in Florida as the Geiger Tree—after John Geiger, a popular sea captain from Key West—this small, shapely tree grows up to 20 feet tall. It is native to the northern coast of South America, Yucatán, the West Indies, and the Florida Keys (where it may have been introduced). Clusters of orange-red flowers are produced several times a year; typically they are at their best in the summer months. The heart-shaped leaves are deep green and are covered with short, stiff hairs. Natives sometimes use the dark, hard, nicely figured wood for small projects, but the tree does not yield enough lumber to make it commercially viable.

*Cordia sebestena*
Geiger Tree

*Cordia sebestena*
Geiger Tree

*Cordia boissieri*
(BOY-see-rye)
This tree is a Mexican native and is also found in Texas (Rio Grande Valley). The common name is Texas Wild Olive because of the olive-size fruit it produces. The Spanish-speaking residents of the valley call it Anacuhuita. Southern Floridians call it White Geiger. White flowers with antique-gold centers are produced in clusters along the branch tips. *Cordia boissieri* is a tree of great promise for Central and South Florida because of its cold tolerance (low 20s or colder). It has a full, rounded shape, grows up to 25 feet tall, and makes a nice lawn ornamental.

*Cordia boissieri*
Texas Wild Olive, White Geiger

*Cordia lutea*
(LOO-tee-a)
This Cordia was introduced to Florida from Ecuador by the USDA. As a small tree growing up to 15 feet tall or as a spreading shrub, it produces clusters of yellow flowers (one inch across) throughout the summer. Rarely offered commercially, it can be seen at Fairchild Tropical Garden in Miami and at Marie Selby Botanical Gardens in Sarasota. The native range of *Cordia lutea* is limited to the dry western regions of Peru, Ecuador, and the Galapagos Islands.

*Cordia lutea*
Yellow Cordia

*Cordia superba*
(soo-PER-ba)
Native to eastern Brazil, this tree looks similar to *Cordia boissieri,* except the flowers are pure white and have more of a delicate, crêpelike appearance. The tree can be obtained from specialty growers in south Florida.

*Cordia superba*
Brazilian Cordia

### Cultivation

Cordia trees produce a fleshy fruit that contains a "pit," similar to a grape or olive. When the fruit is ripe, remove the pit and allow it to dry before planting. Air layering and cuttings are alternate methods. The Geiger Tree is well suited to the dry, alkaline, sandy soils of the Keys and holds up well to salt spray. It is, however, quite sensitive to frost.

*Cordia boissieri* and *Cordia superba* are propagated from dry seed. They will typically bloom when only several feet tall. *Cordia lutea* can develop a leggy appearance and benefits from training. Adding organic supplement to poor soils will also help. Cordia trees must be planted in a well-drained area; they will not tolerate "wet feet."

*Cordia boissieri*
Texas Wild Olive, White Geiger

# Crateva

(kra-TAY-va)
CAPPERACEAE
**Sacred Garlic Pear**

Capers have long been used to flavor sauces, relishes, and other dishes. They are made from the flower buds of a Mediterranean shrub (*Capparis spinosa*) in the Capparidaceae family. This plant, with its white to pale-lilac flowers, has a relative with similar characteristics known as *Crateva,* a small genus of about 15 trees and shrubs native to tropical Africa, Asia, and Madagascar.

### *Crateva religiosa*
(ray-lig-ee-O-sa)

The Sacred Garlic Pear was assigned its species name by Johann Georg Adam Forster (1754-1794). It carries religious significance to the Hindus of northern India. This small tree has three leaflets (trifoliate) at the branch tips. Flowers are about four inches across and have four clawlike petals that open white and take on a yellowish cast as they age. Many long, lilac stamens tipped with gold anthers surround an even longer pistil. The tree is deciduous for several months and bears its flowers in the spring before the new leaves. The fruit is a large, spotted berry that is one to two inches in diameter and

*Crateva religiosa*
Sacred Garlic Pear

contains seeds about one-quarter inch long. Although *Crateva religiosa* is cultivated in Asia, it is very rare in the United States. I had reservations about whether to include it in this book, but as with the genus *Brownea*, I couldn't resist the temptation to include the photos, which were taken at the Fairchild Tropical Garden in Miami. Propagate by cuttings in sand (Hortus III).

*Crateva religiosa*
Sacred Garlic Pear

# Delonix

(di-LOH-niks)
CAESALPINIACEAE
**Royal Poinciana**

*Delonix regia*
Royal Poinciana

While sailing along the coast of Madagascar over 140 years ago, the Dutch botanist Wenceslaus Bojer observed a tree covered with bright scarlet blossoms. Since Bojer's discovery, this tree has been planted throughout the tropical regions of the world and is considered by some to be the most awe-inspiring of any flowering tree.

*Delonix regia*
(RAY-gee-a)

It is known in Florida as Royal Poinciana and in Southeast Asia as Flame of the Forest. The Spanish call it *Framboyan* (flamboyant). This fast-growing tree reaches up to 40 feet tall and branches out to form a wide, graceful canopy. The leaves are bipinnate and are comprised of approximately 1,000 small leaflets. (See leaf comparison photos on page 132.) The flowers have five petals; the "standard" petal is white with red and yellow markings. Colors are most often red or orange-red, but there is also a yellow variety and a rare white one. In Florida, *Delonix regia* blooms between May and August. Since 1937, the city of Miami has paid tribute to this tree by holding an annual Royal Poinciana Festival during the first week of June. (It has been estimated that there are now more Royal Poincianas growing in Miami than in Madagascar.) A large, isolated *Delonix regia,* laden with crimson red blooms and nestled among green foliage, is a sight to remember. Many fine specimens can be seen along US Highway 1 on the way to Key West.

*Delonix regia*
Royal Poinciana

### Cultivation

Royal Poinciana is best grown from seed. After nicking the seed, soak in warm water before planting. Wedge-grafting a mature scion onto a pencil-size sapling is a good way to induce bloom on a young tree. Otherwise, Royal Poinciana can take five to seven years to produce flowers. Plant in a sunny location and allow plenty of room. The roots can be aggressive, so avoid planting this tree near septic tanks or other structures. The eventual size can be controlled by careful pruning. Consulting with a trained arborist on this is a good idea.

Although these trees are planted throughout the Tropics, they do best in a climate that has both dry and wet seasons. They are drought-resistant. I've heard some people call Royal Poinciana a "dirty" tree because of shedding leaves and flowers and the long woody seed pods that hang on the tree over winter. However, many people gladly accept the extra maintenance in exchange for the tree's grace and beauty. Once established, it grows fast and is relatively free of disease and insects. Avoid any container-grown tree that is more than four times the height of its tub. The fast-growing roots will become pot-bound if left too long before transplanting. Due to its sensitivity to frost, this tree is limited to zone 10, but true to the theory of supply and demand, you will find it offered in many zone 9 nurseries. I must confess, I planted one in my yard.

*Delonix regia (yellow form)*
Royal Poinciana

# Erythrina

(e-rith-REE-na)
FABACEAE
**Coral Trees**

The name of this genus is derived from the Greek word *erythros,* meaning "red." Most of its 60-plus species are tropical and deciduous. Several are cultivated for their ornamental flowers, which are pollinated by birds. *Erythrinia'*s characteristic thorns are found on young branches and even on the backs of leaves. The wood is sometimes used for timber, although it is very lightweight.

The southeastern region of the United States has its own native *Erythrina herbacea,* a shrub or small tree that grows wild in South Florida's moist, sandy soils. Its common names are Coral Bean and Cherokee Bean.

*Erythrina herbacea*
Coral Bean

*Erythrina variegata*
Tiger Claw

*Erythrina variegata*
(vair-ee-a-GAH-ta)
This Asian species is noted for its attractive foliage as well as its springtime floral display. The large leaves can be solid green or variegated with cream and yellow veining. The variegated kind is often referred to as *Erythrina variegata* var. *orientalis*. Potentially a large tree (up to 60 feet tall), it more often matures when 20 to 30 feet tall. Common names are Tiger Claw and Indian Coral Tree.

*Erythrina variegata*
Tiger Claw

*Erythrina caffra*
(KAF-ra)
This small tree comes from South Africa, where it is called Kafferboom, which means "red bean." Sometimes grown in Florida, it is a popular tree in southern California (and the official tree of Los Angeles). The photo of *Erythrina caffra* was taken at the Los Angeles International Airport. Blossom colors range from red to orange. The flowers appear before the leaves in the spring and are arranged in umbel-like fashion on branch tips.

*Erythrina caffra*
Kafferboom

*Erythrina crista-galli*
(KRIS-ta-ga-lee)
This is Argentina's national tree. It grows up to 15 feet tall with a gnarled, rugged trunk. It is cultivated as a lawn specimen throughout the Tropics, where the color of foliage and flowers varies due to its wide range. On many mature trees, the leaves are a vibrant green-blue that contrasts nicely with the deep-scarlet flowers.

*Erythrina crista-galli*
Cry Baby Tree

### Cultivation

*Erythrina* can be propagated from cuttings or seeds. The red, hard-shell seeds can be given a tepid water soak for 48 hours prior to planting to speed up germination. Although the seeds are used by Native Americans to make necklaces, they are poisonous and should be kept away from children (some natives use them to make rat poison). These trees like a sunny location with rich, moist soil. *Erythrina caffra*, however, does well in average-to-poor soil with minimal water. *Erythrina crista-galli* can be grown in large pots and pruned to control its size. It will tolerate some frost and can be grown outdoors in zone 9.

*Erythrina crista-galli*
Cry Baby Tree

# Guaiacum

(GWI-ah-kum)
ZYGOPHYLLACEAE
**Lignum Vitae** (lig-num-VIE-tee)

These small trees (under 20 feet tall) come from Mexico, the West Indies, the Florida Keys, and the northern coast of South America. In the spring and again in the fall, numerous blue-violet flowers appear. The five-petal blossoms are about one inch across with ten stamens. The seed pods split open and display two to four orange-red seeds. The tree is especially attractive when flowers and red seeds appear at the same time.

"Guaiacum" comes from the Carib Indian word for "medicine gum"; the sap was used as a medical treatment for various ailments. The common name is Lignum Vitae, Latin for "tree of life." There are five species of Lignum Vitae belonging to the family Zygophyllaceae (see also *Bulnesia arborea*). Two species are native to the United States.

*Guaiacum sanctum*
Lignum Vitae

*Guaiacum sanctum*
(SANK-tum)
This species is native to the Florida Keys. Another American species from southwest Texas along the Mexican border is *Guaiacum angustifolium.*

*Guaiacum officinale*
(oh-fi-shi-NAH-lee)
This tree comes from the West Indies and northern regions of Venezuela and Colombia. The leaves are evergreen, opposite-pinnately compound, and shiny dark green on both sides. The bark is light gray, rough, and fissured. The tree shape is compact with dense foliage, making it an attractive ornamental that is sometimes used by bonsai artists. It can grow up to 20 feet tall with a trunk diameter of one to two feet. The photos on these two pages illustrate the difference between the leaves of *Guaiacum officinale* and those of *Guaiacum sanctum.*

*Guaiacum officinale*
Lignum Vitae

### The Lignum Vitae Story

Native Americans introduced the first European settlers to the medicinal value of Lignum Vitae, as noted by the Spanish explorer Gonzalo Oviedo in his journal in 1514. Along with gold and silver, Lignum Vitae was among the first items to be exported to Europe. Lignum Vitae soon became an important lumber export as well, thanks to its high gum content, which provided a natural lubricant. (Early machines were lubricated with animal fat—a messy and smelly method!) Combined with its physical toughness and outstanding rot resistance, Lignum Vitae was an excellent choice for the fabrication of bearings and pulleys, especially for those used underwater, where lubricants cannot be applied.

Bearings for ship and submarine propellers have been made from Lignum Vitae. A famous clock maker from London used it for gears, claiming his clocks would not need lubrication for 50 years. The hinges on the Erie Canal locks were made from Lignum Vitae and lasted over 100 years. Before the age of plastics, the wood was used to make bowling balls, golf clubs, false teeth, and dozens of other items. Weighing in at around 80 pounds per cubic foot, it's one of the hardest and heaviest woods known. All the natural stands of Lignum Vitae, however, have been harvested nearly to extinction. The tree is protected in Florida, and the wood is regulated in international trade. Large trees, estimated at more than 500 years old, can be seen growing in the state park on Lignum Vitae Key just south of Islamorada. Fortunately for flowering tree enthusiasts, Lignum Vitae is becoming more available at Florida nurseries.

*Guaiacum sanctum (seed)*
Lignum Vitae

### Cultivation

Lignum Vitae in its native environment is a slow grower. It's usually found near coastal regions in poor, rocky soils and consequently has a high tolerance for salt and drought.

As a cultured specimen, Lignum Vitae will grow faster with frequent watering and improved (well-drained) soil. It is easy to grow from seed and has no major pests.

*Guaiacum sanctum*
Lignum Vitae

# Jacaranda

(jak-a-RAN-da)
BIGNONIACEAE
**Jacaranda**

In the plant world, blue flowers are a minority compared to red, yellow, and white. An exception is *Jacaranda*—a genus of about 50 tropical and subtropical trees and shrubs that are world renowned for their showy displays of blue flowers. As the lilac signals springtime in the North, the *Jacaranda* does the same in Florida. Ranging from southern Mexico through South America, the *Jacaranda* was one of the first trees imported to the United States from the Tropics.

The name *Jacaranda* comes from an old word of Portuguese and indigenous Brazilian origin. In Brazil, the name is sometimes used to describe the famous "Rio" rosewood lumber, *Dalbergia nigra,* as both these trees have fine, fernlike foliage. This has led to some confusion, because true *Jacaranda* wood is lightweight and has little commercial value. It is best to plant this tree for its flowering beauty!

*Jacaranda mimosifolia*
Jacaranda

## *Jacaranda mimosifolia*
(mi-mo-si-FO-lee-a)

This species from northwest Argentina is the most common variety found in the United States. It grows up to 40 feet tall with long, upright branches. The leaves are deciduous, bipinnate, and compound; they reach 15 to 20 inches in length. Leaflets are pointed and about one-quarter inch long. (See leaf comparison photos on page 133.) Forty to 80 flowers are borne on pyramidal panicles that stand upright or droop on lower branches. Color ranges from sky-blue to purple-blue. There is also a pure white cultivar, *Jacaranda mimosifolia* "Alba." *Jacaranda acutifolia* is sometimes listed as a synonym of *Jacaranda mimosifolia*, but A. H. Gentry and Dr. Edwin Menninger have listed this Peruvian tree as a distinct species.

*Jacaranda mimosifolia*
Jacaranda

*Jacaranda cuspidifolia*
(kus-pi-di-FO-lee-a)
A close relative of *Jacaranda mimosifolia,* this species has larger flowers and longer leaflets (one-half inch). The flower color ranges from blue to blue-violet.

*Jacaranda cuspidifolia*
Jacaranda

*Jacaranda jasminoides*
(jas-min-OY-deez)
This is a small tree that grows up to 20 feet tall and is native to southern Mexico. Leaves are bipinnate. The leaflets are soft, downy, and much larger than those of most Jacarandas. Flower buds are dark purple and flowers, red-purple. Rare in Florida, this is a nice variety for those who are looking for something different.

### Cultivation

Jacaranda is grown from seed or from softwood cuttings. As a sapling, it is often staked and pruned to improve form. Cultivars are typically grafted onto *Jacaranda mimosifolia* rootstock. Growth rate is moderate. Jacaranda is drought-tolerant but will benefit from frequent watering during the summer. Plant in full sun in well-drained soil. Jacaranda blooms younger and more prolifically in central Florida than in south Florida. The reason for this is not known, but speculation is that cool winter nights are required to promote spring bloom. Mature trees will take several degrees of frost, and trees that have been badly damaged by a freeze often return vigorously from the roots. The best Jacarandas I've seen are prominently displayed at the entrance to the Epcot Center at Walt Disney World in Orlando.

*Jacaranda jasminoides*
Maroon Jacaranda

# Koelreuteria

(kurl-roy-TAIR-ee-a)
SAPINDACEAE
**Golden Rain Tree**

This genus of about four species was named by Erik Laxmann in honor of Joseph Koelreuter (1733-1806), professor of natural history at Karlsruhe (Germany) and a pioneer in the study of hybridization. These deciduous trees originate from China; three species are cultivated in the United States. *Koelreuteria*, like several other genera in this book, uses the big-bang approach to reproduction. The trees bloom only once a year, but their display is intense. Flowers, which are produced in showy panicles above the foliage, often cover the tree. The small yellow petals that fall to the ground en masse inspired the common name Golden Rain Tree. Following bloom, bladderlike seed capsules are produced containing three round, black seeds. These two-inch-long capsules appear salmon or red before turning tan-brown and hang on the tree like Chinese paper lanterns for several months. Its fragrant flowers and colorful seed pods make this tree a desirable ornamental.

*Koelreuteria bipinnate*
Golden Rain Tree

*Koelreuteria bipinnate*
(bie-pi-NAH-ta)
This tree is native to the southwestern regions of China. Its 9 to 16 leaves are bipinnate, about 4 inches long, and 1 1/2 inches wide. The leaflets are partially or unequally serrate. Flowers have five petals, and bloom occurs around September. This species is hardy throughout Florida (zone 8).

*Koelreuteria bipinnate*
Golden Rain Tree

### Koelreuteria elegans
(EL-i-ganz)

A close relative of *Koereuteria bipinnate,* this tree is native to east China and Taiwan. Its 7 to 12 leaves are bi-pinnate, about 4 inches long, and 1 1/2 inches wide. The entire perimeter of the leaflet is serrate. Flowers have four petals, and bloom occurs around September. This tree can be grown north of Florida to zone 7.

### Koelreuteria paniculata
(pan-ik-ew-LAH-ta)

This hardy Golden Rain Tree is native to northern China and Korea. Leaves are pinnate (sometimes bipinnate). Leaflets number from 12 to 18, are about 5 inches long and 2 1/2 inches wide, and are crenate-serrate (with small, rounded teeth). Flowers have four petals (solid yellow), and bloom occurs around May (a cultivar called "September" blooms in late summer). This tree is the most widely cultivated species because of its freeze tolerance to zone 5.

### Cultivation

*Koelreuteria elegans* and *Koelreuteria bipinnate*, more suited to a subtropical climate, are typically found in central and south Florida. They are nearly identical in form and habit. Golden Rain Trees are easy to grow from seed, and seedlings are often found growing under adult trees or in nearby flower beds. The growth rate is moderate to fast. Trees reach a height of about 40 feet and require little pruning. They do best in a sunny location but will tolerate light shade. As saplings, they require moist soil, either acid or alkaline, but once established, they can withstand drought. Roots grow deep and are noninvasive.

*Koelreuteria bipinnate (seed pods)*
Golden Rain Tree

# Lagerstroemia

(lah-ger-STROH-mee-a)
LYTHRACEAE
**Crape Myrtle, Queens Crape Myrtle**

*Lagerstroemia* is named for Swedish botanist Magnus Von Lagerstroem, who collected Indian plants for Carl Linnaeus. Known throughout the southeastern United States as Crape Myrtle, *Lagerstroemia* can be recognized by its outstanding summer blooms of delicate crinkled petals.

### Lagerstroemia indica

(IN-di-ka)
This is a much hybridized species common from North Carolina southward. Shapes range from bushy shrubs to small- and medium-size trees. The leaves are two to three inches long and are elliptical or obovate. The trunk is smooth and mottled, with some shedding occurring in the winter when the tree is deciduous. Flower colors include white, pink, lavender, and red.

*Lagerstroemia indica* originated in China. Many of Florida's outstanding imported plants come from China, which is not surprising when you consider that over 25 percent of this vast country lies in the same temperate zones as Florida. There are perhaps 15 to 20 species of *Lagerstroemia* that are native to the tropical regions of Southeast Asia.

*Lagerstroemia indica*
Crape Myrtle

*Lagerstroemia speciosa*
(spee-see-O-sa)
This species is the most cultivated of the tropical group. Common names are Pride of India and Queens Crape Myrtle. It is also called *Lagerstroemia flos-reginae.* The color is sometimes light pink or magenta but is most often lavender. The typical blossom opens during the night as a dark, vibrant lavender, then fades to a lighter shade and drops after three to four days. The inflorescence is a tall spike

*Lagerstroemia speciosa*
Queens Crape Myrtle

one to two feet long above the leaves. Blooming starts at the base and can continue for several weeks. Woody fruits (round pods one inch across) can remain on the tree throughout the winter. The leaves are 6 to 12 inches long and are oblong or lanceolate. In India, the tree can reach 80 feet in height and provides a valuable timber called "Jarool." The hard and durable reddish wood is used for fine cabinetry and exterior applications. Most trees in Florida do not exceed 30 feet in height because they lack the jungle canopy that would promote taller growth.

*Lagerstroemia speciosa*
Queens Crape Myrtle

*Lagerstroemia loudonii*
(loo-DON-eye)
This tree, a native of Thailand and
Cambodia, is a close relative of

*Lagerstroemia speciosa*. It was photographed at Fairchild Tropical Garden in Miami.

*Lagerstroemia loudonii*
Tropical Crape Myrtle

*Lagerstroemia floribunda*
(flo-ri-BUN-da)
This Malaysian tree is another close relative to *Lagerstroemia speciosa*. One report indicates that it is more evergreen in Florida, where it sometimes provides a second bloom in November.

### Cultivation

*Lagerstroemia* needs ample water and a sunny location to do its best. Drought will cause leaf burn and inhibit bloom. *Lagerstroemia indica* should be pruned back hard in February. Remove base suckers periodically. I prefer to establish a trunk of one to three main stems pruned up to four to six feet, but this is a matter of personal taste. Powdery white mildew is sometimes a problem on shaded, moist leaves. Treat with a fungicide. Mildew-resistant cultivars have been introduced recently.

Tropical *Lagerstroemia* seed is noted for its lack of fertility. Use fresh seed and try different sources. Older Queens Crape Myrtles can withstand a light frost, but saplings are badly damaged or killed by freezing temperatures.

*Lagerstroemia floribunda*
Tropical Crape Myrtle

# Lonchocarpus

(lon-cho-KAR-pus)
FABACEAE
**Lance Pod**

This genus of more than 100 species is native to tropical America, Africa, and Australia and was named by German botanist Carl Kunth in 1824. It is known for its ornamental displays of white, mauve, or violet sweet pea–shaped flowers.

*Lonchocarpus violaceus*
(vie-oh-LAY-see-us)
This beautiful small tree from the Caribbean came to Florida via Fairchild Tropical Garden. This evergreen tree produces a wide, spreading canopy to a height of 20 feet. It blooms in the fall with copious spikes of mauve flowers above the foliage. The seed is produced in long, slender pods, hence its common name, Lance Pod. Another name used is *Lonchocarpus punctatus*. Some species of *Lonchocarpus*, along with their African relatives *Bolusanthus* and *Millettia*, can grow large and produce valuable timber. The attractive African wood "wenge" is produced from *Millettia laurentii*.

*Lonchocarpus violaceus*
Lance Pod

### Cultivation

*Lonchocarpus violaceus* is grown from seed, although it does not produce seed in great quantity. It has a moderate growth rate and prefers an enriched, moist soil. As this tree is frost-sensitive, central Floridians may want to consider a close relative, *Bolusanthus speciosus*. Sometimes called Rhodesian Wisteria or Rhodesian Teak, *Bolusanthus speciosus* is deciduous and has some frost resistance. It produces violet flowers in the early spring. Plant *Bolusanthus* when young, because the growth rate is very slow in pots.

*Lonchocarpus violaceus*
Lance Pod

# Nerium

(NAY-ree-um)
APOCYNACEAE
**Oleander**

One of the most adaptable plants available in tropical and subtropical areas is Oleander. Often referred to as tall shrubs, some hybrids are easily trained into trees with full crowns and lots of color. Perhaps due to its popularity as a shrub, its potential as a tree form is often overlooked. Oleander originated in Mediterranean coastal regions, which explains its tolerance for salt.

### *Nerium oleander*
(o-lee-AN-der)

Oleander has pointed oblong or lanceolate leaves that can grow up to ten inches long. Flowers are either single or double. Many available cultivars produce red, pink, cream, or white flowers. Trade names such as "Sister Agnes" and "Mrs. Roeding" are commonly used to identify them. If you are purchasing a sapling to train as a tree, you'll want to inquire about the plant's adult size. Many oleanders, such as "Petite Pink," are referred to as dwarf varieties and will grow from only two to four feet tall.

*Nerium oleander*
Oleander

*Nerium oleander*
Oleander

### Cultivation

Oleander grows in almost any soil, including soil with a high salt content. It prefers a sunny location for best bloom. Its temperature rating varies, but most hybrids do well down to 20° F or even colder. Oleander will take a good deal of shearing, which is needed to shape the tree and also to improve bloom. Since oleander often blooms continuously from spring until fall, heavy pruning is best done in late winter. Propagate from cuttings or air layering.

There is one important feature about oleander to note: All parts of the plant are toxic to humans and animals if ingested. History books document a case where soldiers of Napoleon's army died after cooking their meal over a spit made of oleander. Precautions should be made to limit exposure to clippings or flowers that are brought inside for display. Another problem is the oleander caterpillar. These orange pests are easily controlled with insecticides such as Lindane or Sevin.

*Nerium oleander*
Oleander

*Nerium oleander*
Oleander

# Parkinsonia

(park-in-SOWN-ee-a)
CAESALPINIACEAE
**Jerusalem Thorn**

This genus of several species was named for botanical author John Parkinson (1567-1650).

*Parkinsonia aculeata*
(a-kew-lee-AH-ta)
This small tree is native to Mexico, the West Indies, and the northern parts of South America. It is widely cultivated and is now considered naturalized in the American Southwest and in Florida. Sometimes growing to 20 feet tall, it has green branches with one-inch spikes. The common name in Florida is Jerusalem Thorn, which is believed to signify the crown of thorns worn by Christ. Leaves are pinnate; leaflets are loosely spaced on flattened twigs. The tree is deciduous during winter or during prolonged drought, when it photosynthesizes through its green limbs. Fragrant, yellow flowers are produced in long clusters during the spring and periodically throughout the summer. *Parkinsonia floridum* (Blue Paloverde) and *Parkinsonia microphylla* (Yellow Paloverde) are related species growing in the arid regions of the American Southwest and Mexico. They are more often listed under the genus *Cercidium* and are rarely cultivated outside their native range.

*Parkinsonia aculeata*
Jerusalem Thorn

### Cultivation

Propagate this fast-growing tree from seed. It prefers a sunny location and is not particular to any soil type as long as the soil is well drained. It will tolerate periodic wet conditions but can develop root rot if planted in a damp area. When the tree is mature, prune low limbs and spikes for safety. Jerusalem Thorn makes a nice lawn ornamental and provides seasonal color with a delicate, transparent look.

*Parkinsonia aculeata*
Jerusalem Thorn

# Peltophorum

(pel-TOF-or-um)
CAESALPINIACEAE
**Copper Pod, Peltophorum**

An excellent, fast-growing tree for summer color and shade is *Peltophorum*. Unfortunately, vernacular names such as Yellow Poinciana and Yellow Jacaranda have created mass confusion over the identity of this tree. The Latin name *Peltophorum* is not difficult to pronounce and suits the tree best.

### *Peltophorum pterocarpum*
(te-ro-KAR-pum)
Also known as *Peltophorum inerme,* this tree originated in the Philippine Islands. Popular in south Florida, it's a medium-size tree (30 to 40 feet tall) and produces a dense crown of dark green foliage. Upright spikes of yellow flowers are produced from May through August. It seems to adapt well to urban conditions and is used extensively as a street tree in Singapore and in the Malaysian capital of Kuala Lumpur. The buds and young stems are covered with rust-colored tomenta (velvet hairs). The reddish-brown seed pods look like smooth copper. Leaves are bipinnate, and leaflets are about 3/4 of an inch long and are arranged in 10 to 20 pairs.

*Peltophorum pterocarpus*
Copper Pod

*Peltophorum dubium*
Peltophorum

*Peltophorum dubium*
(DOO-bee-um)
This a medium-size tree that comes from eastern and southern Brazil (also Uruguay and Paraguay). It looks very similar to *Peltophorum pterocarpum* but is more cold toler-ant, making it the tree of choice for central Florida. The flower buds are golden rather than rust-colored, and the seeds are a dull gray-tan. Leaflets are about 1/2 inch long and are ar-ranged in 20 to 30 pairs. (See leaf comparison photos on page 132.) This tree blooms in the summer, but the amount of bloom is unpredict-able. I've seen trees produce a flush of bright, golden bloom one year and little or nothing the following year. This seems to be a characteristic of the tree, not the climate. Central Florida trees lose most, if not all, of their leaves in the winter.

*Peltophorum dubium*
Peltophorum

*Peltophorum africanum*
(af-ri-KAH-num) is a rare offering in Florida nurseries. It's almost identical to *Peltophorum pterocarpum* but has more fragrant flowers and rarely grows taller than 30 feet.

### Cultivation
*Peltophorum* is easy to grow from seed. It is a virtually maintenance-free tree that requires no staking as a sapling and only occasional pruning when mature. It has good drought tolerance, and its pleasant fragrance and brightly colored blossoms are sought after for indoor flower arrangements.

*Peltophorum dubium*
Peltophorum

# Sesbania

(ses-BAY-nee-a)
FABACEAE
**Rattle Box, Red Wisteria**

*Sesbania* is a genus of several tropical and subtropical trees from Australia, Asia, Africa, and North and South America. They are noted for their fast growth rate and their pendulous racemes of ornamental flowers.

*Sesbania punicea*
(poo-NEE-see-a)
This is a small tree or shrub native to Uruguay, Paraguay, and southern Brazil that has been naturalized in Florida. The brilliant red or red-orange pealike flowers can be seen from a long distance. Its common name is Rattle Box because of its long pods that house numerous seeds that rattle in the wind. It is sometimes found growing along the roadside. In some parts of the world it's called Red Wisteria. It was formerly classified under the genus *Daubentonia. Sesbania tripetti* is listed as a synonym in the USDA-GRIN database.

**Cultivation**
*Sesbania* is a very fast grower from seed. Left to grow unattended, *Sesbania punicea* will grow into a large shrub with long, drooping branches. It can, however, be trained to have a heavy trunk. Rarely offered in nurseries (probably due to the training requirements), *Sesbania punicea* is a good choice if you are looking for vibrant red-orange color. *Sesbania grandiflora* is a close relative that assumes more of a tree stature. Maintain an adequate water supply. The seeds are poisonous and present some concern to livestock owners.

*Sesbania punicea*
Rattle Box

# Spathodea

(spa-THO-dee-a)
BIGNONIACEAE
**African Tulip Tree**

Equatorial Africa is known for its vast tracks of lush vegetation. Pushing themselves above the canopy, providing a striking contrast to the greenery, are the fiery blooms of the African Tulip Tree.

### *Spathodea campanulata*

(kam-PAN-yew-la-ta)
This fascinating tree was first described by A. M. F. Palisot de Beauvois in 1787. Palisot de Beauvois named the genus from the Greek word *spathe*, or "broadsword," for its curved calyx. He named the species from the Latin *campanulatus,* meaning "bell-shaped," for its flower. *Spathodea campanulata* is native to central Africa, from Sierra Leone and Liberia through Zaire and Uganda. Although it's sometimes found in the jungle, where it can reach 80 feet tall, it prefers the surrounding open forests where it has more room and only grows to 30 or 40 feet tall. The flowers are ar-

*Spathodea campanulata*
Africa Tulip Tree

ranged on branch tips, and the buds are grouped in circular fashion. If squeezed, these buds will send a stream of water out the end, to the amusement of children. Over time, the buds on the perimeter open to display the flowers richly colored in shades of red and orange with a yellow fringe. A solid yellow variation exists, but it is uncommon. After a day or two, the flowers drop and are replaced by the next row of buds. Flowering can continue this way for weeks. The fruits are boat-shaped capsules containing hundreds of small, papery seeds. In Florida, the African Tulip Tree blooms two or three times a year starting in the spring. It is evergreen in south Florida and semideciduous in central Florida. The wood is soft and somewhat brittle and has been used by native Africans for making drums. Dr. Edwin Menninger reported that the tree's seed-producing capability is unpredictable. Some trees produce an abundant crop then do not produce for years later. Some trees never produce seed.

*Spathodea campanulata*
Africa Tulip Tree

### Cultivation

African Tulip Trees are propagated from seed or cuttings. Seedlings require constant warmth; even mature trees are quite frost-sensitive. These trees prefer a sunny location in sandy loam soil with adequate water. Occasional applications of fertilizer will help keep the leaves a deep green color. Seedlings quickly develop a strong trunk and rarely require staking; tree form is upright. These trees are not noted for keeping an attractive shape as they age, but pruning when young will help maintain form. The most striking African Tulip Tree I've seen is only two miles from my central Florida home. This 10-year-old tree is about 20 feet high and 20 feet wide. It's a prolific bloomer with a nice shape that results from the natural pruning process of winter frosts. A hard freeze will typically kill these trees to the ground, but like *Jacaranda*, they can quickly regenerate from the roots.

*Spathodea campanulata*
African Tulip Tree

# Tabebuia

(tab-a-BOO-ee-a)
BIGNONIACEAE
**Trumpet Trees**

*Tabebuia* is an old Brazilian name given to this highly regarded group of flowering trees. Its wide variation in color, size, and shape makes *Tabebuia* an interesting and sometimes confusing genus. Common attributes include opposite, palmately compound leaves and trumpet-shaped flowers, for which they are often referred to as Trumpet Trees. There are more than 150 species of *Tabebuia*—native to Central and South America, but only about a dozen—not all of which are found in Florida nurseries—produce spectacular blooms. The literature is full of contradictions on the classification of *Tabebuia*. Alwyn Gentry, a world renowned expert in Bignoniaceae, provided a comprehensive treatment of *Tabebuia* in *Flora Neotropica*, Number 25, published by the New York Botanical Garden in 1992.

*Tabebuia argentea*
Silver Tabebuia, Tree of Gold

*Tabebuia argentea*
Silver Tabebuia, Tree of Gold

One method of classifying *Tabebuia* is by its wood. Timber experts recognize three wood types: a very hard, dense wood that resembles Lignum Vitae (*Guaiacum*) and is commercially viable; a medium-hard wood that resembles oak; and a soft wood that resembles cedar. The trees that follow are listed by wood type.

### Dense-Wood Species

The dense-wood group includes several species now being cultivated in Florida. In addition to being hard, the wood is highly decay-resistant and is used for exterior and marine applications. Another name for this group is *Lapacho,* a Spanish word also used for the oil produced from the sap.

#### *Tabebuia chrysotricha*
(kris-oh-TRI-ka)
This yellow flowering species is native to Colombia and Brazil. The shape of the tree is often open-crown. The bloom cycle is relatively short (between three and five weeks) but intense. This occurs around March, when the trees are bare. Most *Tabebuias* start to bloom at only one to two years of age. On mature specimens, dense bloom clusters are produced at the branch tips and cover the tree in a vivid golden mass. Truly spectacular! Long, tubelike seed pods appear after bloom. *Tabebuia chrysotricha* can be identified by its hairy seed pods and by its young twigs, which are covered with a brown velvet.

*Tabebuia chrysotricha*
Golden Trumpet Tree

*Tabebuia chrysotricha*
Golden Trumpet Tree

*Tabebuia chrysotricha (seed pods)*
Golden Trumpet Tree

*Tabebuia chrysantha*
(kris-ANTH-a)
This species is a close relative to
*Tabebuia chrysotricha* and is native to
areas from Mexico to Venezuela. The
leaves are narrower and more
pointed than *Tabebuia chrysotricha*,
and the seed pods are thin-walled,
longer, and less hairy.

*Tabebuia umbellata*
(um-bel-AH-ta)
From the coastal regions of Brazil
comes another close relative of
*Tabebuia chrysotricha*.

This small yellow flowering tree is
usually not more than 15 feet tall
and tends to grow with a wide
crown. In its native range, it is often
found in swampy areas. The fruits
can be very long—up to 20
inches—and have little or no hair.
*Tabebuia umbellata* has survived
temperatures in the low 20s, making
it one of the most cold-hardy of the
*Tabebuia*s. The other trees listed in
the *Lapacho* group have some frost
and freeze tolerance to the mid-20s.

*Tabebuia chrysantha*
Golden Trumpet Tree

*Tabebuia umbellata*
Golden Trumpet Tree

*Tabebuia umbellata*
Golden Trumpet Tree

*Tabebuia ochracea*
(ok-RAH-see-a)
A rare find in Florida, this species is cultivated in Central and South America. The tree in the photo was taken at the former home of David Fairchild (The Kampong) in late May, long after other *Tabebuia*s had finished their bloom cycles. Gentry described a sample taken from Buenos Aires: "Tree to 18m (58 feet), flowers yellow with reddish nectar guides."

*Tabebuia ochracea*
Golden Trumpet Tree

*Tabebuia ochracea*
Golden Trumpet Tree

*Tabebuia impetiginosa*
(im-pe-ti-gi-NOH-sa)
A very nice lavender flowering tree from South America is Ipe. The flowers can also be found in shades from pink to rose. Some experts list *Tabebuia avellanedae* and *Tabebuia palmeri* as synonyms for this tree. The predictable bloom cycle lasts from early February through late March. From a distance, the flowers produce a magenta cast over the crown, but on close inspection you can see that the throats and bottom petals are variegated with yellow. Ipe has smooth, gray bark that becomes fissured on older trees. The leaves have serrated edges. This attractive tree rarely exceeds 30 feet in height on Florida lawns and deserves wider use in home landscaping.

*Tabebuia impetiginosa*
Ipe

*Tabebuia serratifolia*
(ser-at-i-FOH-lee-a)
This is a large timber tree that has serrated leaves similar to *Tabebuia impetiginosa* and blooms yellow. The wood that comes from these two species is marketed under the name Ipe. Woodworkers may also find this exotic lumber advertised as Pau d'Arco.

*Tabebuia serratifolia*
Golden Ipe

*Tabebuia heptaphylla*
(hep-ta-FIL-a)
This pink-lavender flowering tree is a close relative of *Tabebuia impetiginosa* but has seed pods that are thinner (less than one half inch wide) and less woody. It can grow fairly large (about 50 feet tall).

*Tabebuia heptaphylla*
Ipe

## Medium-Hard Wood Species

The second group, characterized by medium-hard wood, is often referred to as the *Roble* (Spanish for "oak") group.

### *Tabebuia pallida*
(PA-li-da)

This semideciduous or evergreen *Tabebuia* from the West Indies is popular in south Florida, where it is less likely to encounter a freeze. Its flowers are light pink or nearly white and contrast nicely with its dark green foliage, although some trees shed their leaves just before the spring bloom. Tree shape is similar to a Scotch pine or fir, and leaves are smooth with an oily sheen. The arrangement of flowers is singular or in small groups. The common name is Cuban Tabebuia.

*Tabebuia pallida*
Cuban Tabebuia

### Soft-Wood Species

The third group, with wood that resembles cedar, includes most of the *Tabebuia* species. Few of these are cultivated; however, one species has become very popular in the United States.

### Tabebuia argentea
(ar-GEN-tee-a)
This is the most common *Tabebuia* grown in Florida. Blooming in dense umbel clusters, it can put on a striking display of golden yellow blossoms. Like *Tabebuia chrysotricha*, the bloom cycle is relatively short but comes at a time when the tourist season is at its peak. The tree is most easily identified by its puffy, fissured, corklike bark. Its branches often grow with irregular curving patterns, giving the tree an interesting shape. This tree is sometimes referred to as the Tree of Gold or Silver Trumpet Tree.

The name *argentea,* meaning "silver," refers to the silver cast of young foliage and branches. This has been the most common name found in literature, but an older name, *Tabebuia caraiba*, is used frequently. The oldest name, *Tabebuia aurea*, given by Antonio Luiz Patricio Da Silva Manso (1788-1818), is used by Gentry and the USDA-GRIN database.

I like using the name Silver Tabebuia because it helps distinguish this tree from the other yellow flowering species.

*Tabebuia argentea*
Silver Tabebuia

### Cultivation

Trumpet trees are easy to grow and require very little maintenance. They have no major pests and are tolerant of many different soil types, although an enriched sandy soil is best (pH of 5.5 to 7.0). Rust disease can develop on the leaves but rarely to any significant degree. Young trees, especially *Tabebuia argentea,* may require support and training. They can tolerate a long drought and can also withstand short periods of wet soil.

Growth rate is moderate. *Tabebuia* has some salt tolerance but is generally not recommended for beachside planting.

*Tabebuia* deserves a wider distribution in Florida. It's a good shade tree and has a better cold tolerance than most "subtropicals." It was a pink flowering *Tabebuia* in his hometown of Stuart that prompted Dr. Edwin Menninger to call it "the most beautiful flowering tree I have ever seen."

*Tabebuia argentea*
Silver Tabebuia

# Tecoma

(te-KOH-ma)
BIGNONIACEAE
**Yellow Elder**

Derived from a native Mexican word, *Tecoma* was the name given to this genus of small trees and shrubs by Antoine Laurent de Jussieu (1748-1836). Jussieu also named the genus *Jacaranda* and the "trumpet-flower" family *Bignoniaceae*.

*Tecoma stans*
(STANZ)
The flower of this tree is the official flower of the United States Virgin Islands and the Bahamas. In addition to the West Indies, *Tecoma stans* is also native to Mexico and the

*Tecoma stans*
Yellow Elder

*Tecoma stans*
Yellow Elder

northern parts of South America. It is now considered naturalized in the southern parts of Florida, Texas, and Arizona. Known in Florida as Yellow Elder, this bushy shrub can reach 20 feet tall; if trained as a tree form, it can develop a trunk up to 1 foot in diameter. The bark is light gray and fissured on older specimens. Leaves are pinnate; leaflets are about four to five inches long, are serrated, and come to a point. Color is light to medium green. Flowers are yellow and trumpet-shaped and are borne on upright panicles that can produce up to 60 blossoms! These blooms produce an enticing aroma, but look inside the corolla before you sniff: These flowers attract a host of beings besides humans, including bees, butterflies, and hummingbirds.

Yellow Elder is semideciduous and has a moderate bloom in the spring after new leaves appear. The big spectacle comes in September, when it blooms profusely for two to three weeks. Cylindrical seed pods about the size of a pencil follow bloom.

## Cultivation

Propagate from seeds, which readily germinate. These plants adapt to a wide variety of soils. They can withstand drought but prosper from adequate water during the summer. Flowering can occur the first year. Yellow Elder takes a bit of training to look its best: It tends to sucker at the base and will appear leggy and ragged if left unattended. Seedlings require staking. Once a trunk develops, prune back hard to obtain a full crown. This can be done in late winter before new leaves appear and again in early summer, which allows for new growth before fall bloom. For indoor floral displays, crush and split the stems before placing in deep water.

Yellow Elder will take some frost but not without some damage. It is suitable for beachside planting. Dr. Edwin Menninger wrote about a species from Ecuador, *Tecoma gaudichaudii*. He reported that this tree, which at first glance looks very similar to *Tecoma stans*, requires much less training and blooms year-round.

# Tibouchina

(ti-boo-CHEE-na)
MELASTOMATACEAE
**Tibouchina**

*Tibouchina* is the native name given to this genus of more than 300 species by French botanist Jean Baptiste Aublet (1720-1778). It was another Frenchman, Celestin Alfred Cogniaux (1841-1916), who named many of the species currently in cultivation. Mostly Brazilian in origin, *Tibouchina* is noted for showy displays of purple flowers. A few species are ranked among the most outstanding of flowering trees.

### *Tibouchina granulosa*

(gran-you-LOH-sa)

The Purple Glory Tree is grown in the warm regions of California and Florida. A bushy tree that can grow to 40 feet tall, it blooms twice a year, in the spring around March and again in midsummer. A third bloom sometimes occurs in the fall. Flowering panicles at branch tips can cover the tree with rich, velvetlike blossoms. Leaves are dark green and stiff with sparse hairs on top and bristly hairs on the ribs underneath. Branches are four-sided with wings at each corner. A panoramic display of towering hedges and single-tree specimens can be seen at Cypress Gardens in Winter Haven, Florida.

*Tibouchina granulosa*
Purple Glory Tree

*Tibouchina urvilleana*
(ur-vil-ee-AN-a)
This shrub or treelet grows up to 15 feet tall and makes a nice garden plant. It was named after the French naval officer Jules d'Urville. Young branches are covered with reddish brown pilose (soft hairs). Leaves are soft to the touch. The common name is Princess Flower.

*Tibouchina grandifolia*
(gran-di-FOH-lee-a)
This Tibouchina shrub was photographed at Harry P. Leu Gardens in Orlando, Florida. Reaching six to seven feet high, the flowers are arranged on one-foot vertical spikes. The leaves are very similar to those of *Tibouchina urvilleana* in color and texture, except they are larger and much wider (about three to four inches wide).

### Cultivation
Grow from seed or cuttings in moist, sandy loam soil. Soil should be kept acidic (pH 5.5 to 6.5). Fertilize after bloom. *Tibouchina urvilleana* can be pruned back hard in winter or periodically during the year to prevent a leggy appearance. *Tibouchina* does not grow well in the alkaline soils of south Florida and must be protected from freezing temperatures in other locations. Potted specimens are great for patios.

*Tibouchina urvilleana*
Princess Flower

*Tibouchina grandifolia*
Tibouchina

# Tipuana

(ti-poo-AH-na)
FABACEAE
**Tipu, Pride of Bolivia**

Along the foothills of the Bolivian Andes grows a beautiful yellow flowering tree called Tipu. It is also referred to as Pride of Bolivia. I first encountered this tree growing at the Walt Disney World Resort in Orlando, Florida, where dozens of large trees provide tourists with shade and color. In Florida, the bloom cycle starts in the spring and continues throughout the summer, with peak bloom from late spring to early summer.

*Tipuana tipu*
(TI-poo)
Tipu has flowers that are about three-fourths of an inch long and that, on close inspection, resemble a miniature orchid. The tree is a source of timber in Bolivia and is sometimes referred to as "rosewood," although the lumber looks more like American ash (*Fraxinus*). Tipu was a favorite of Kate Sessions, who was famous for the many trees she planted in San Diego during the early 1900s. The tree is also cultivated in southern France and Argentina. The leaves are light green and bipinnate, with leaflets about one and a half inches long. They provide medium shade and are semideciduous.

*Tipuana tipu*
Tipu

### Cultivation

Tipu is easily propagated from seed. Seeds are in the shape of a winged key (similar to half of a maple tree seed). Seedlings grow rapidly, six to nine feet the first year. As saplings, these trees need support and training. I call Tipu the "ugly duckling tree" because of its gangly appearance when young. Once in the ground, however, it quickly develops into a beautiful tree with a broad crown. In Florida, these trees do well in sandy loam with adequate drainage. They are not salt-tolerant and do not like alkaline soil. Disney has demonstrated that Tipu—hardy to zone 9—deserves much wider use in Florida.

*Tipuana tipu*
Tipu

*Delonix regia*
Royal Poinciana

*Peltophorum dubium*
Peltophorum

*Albizia julibrissin*
Silk Tree

*Jacaranda mimosifolia*
Jacaranda

# Selecting and Planting a Flowering Tree

Whether you're growing trees from seed or buying large specimens from commercial growers, trees can be a substantial investment. Knowing as much as possible about the characteristics and preferences of the trees you choose will help you get the best results. Here are some factors to consider.

## Soil pH

Most flowering trees prefer a soil that is slightly acidic. Some parts of Florida, particularly coastal regions, have soil that is on the alkaline side. When in doubt, have your soil tested. Trees that will accept alkaline soils include *Cordia sebestena*, *Guaiacum sanctum*, *Delonix regia*, and *Caesalpinia vesicaria*.

## Soil nutrients

Florida soils are typically nutrient-poor, resulting in yellowing leaves and an overall sickly appearance. A few trees like *Cochlospermum* can do well in these conditions, but for most, periodic application of fertilizer is required. *Bauhinia* is a genus that requires heavy feeding.

## Soil moisture

Soil and elevation that provide good drainage are usually best. However, some trees may prefer wet or dry soil. Knowing the climate of the trees' native habitat will remove any guesswork.

## Training requirements

In their natural state, *Nerium oleander*, *Tecoma stans*, and *Cassia bicapsularis* are large shrubs. Getting them into tree form involves staking and periodic pruning. *Tipuana tipu* is an unruly youngster that, when given some help, grows into an attractive adult.

## Maintenance

All living things shed something. Trees shed bark, leaves, seeds, and flowers (some more than others). Flowering trees sometimes present a trade-off between ornamental beauty and slightly higher maintenance requirements. Another maintenance task may be insect control.

## Salt tolerance

Living within sight of the ocean creates some tough growing conditions. Salt spray is detrimental to most flowering trees. *Nerium*, *Delonix*, *Guaiacum*, and *Tecoma* are exceptions. Irrigation water in Florida may also contain enough salt to damage foliage.

## Size

Landscaping is often compared to painting a picture: There are foreground, background, and subjects. The main difference is that it may take a number of years for your "picture" to mature. Knowing the adult size of each plant will allow you to visualize the final result. Overcrowding will push trees up where blooms are out of sight.

## Cold tolerance

Only a small percentage of Florida real estate is frost-free. Key West is the only major city that has never recorded freezing temperatures. However, if your area has a commercial citrus industry, you can probably grow most of the trees in this book. Become familiar with the risks, and plant accordingly.

## Wind tolerance

Soft-wooded trees such as *Jacaranda*, *Spathodea*, and *Erythrina* sometimes fall prey to gusty Florida winds. Pruning long, leggy branches helps to shape these tree and prevents limbs from breaking in storms.

## Growth rate

Good news for the impatient gardener: Trees such as *Peltophorum*, *Delonix*, and *Spathodea* can grow from seed to eight-foot saplings in less than two years. Once in the ground, they can reach maturity a few years later. Certain species of *Bauhinia*, *Tecoma*, and *Tabebuia* can bloom the first year from seed while in pots.

# Temperature Trends

Cold damage is always a concern to the tropical plant enthusiast in Florida. *Delonix regia* and *Bauhinia monondra*, for example, are high-risk trees if your area has any frost. However, many trees in this book will withstand temperatures of 25° to 32° F for several hours without major damage. Temperatures below 25° F often spell disaster, not only for ornamental growers but also for the commercial citrus industry, which has multimillion-dollar crops at stake.

The following charts were made from a database of daily minimum temperatures from 1948 through 1996. The data was recorded at major airports in Orlando, Tampa, West Palm Beach, and Miami and was made available to the public by the National Oceanic and Atmospheric Administration (NOAA) via its World Wide Web site.

The first two charts on the opposite page illustrate the number of days freezing temperatures were recorded at the four aforementioned locations in Florida, summed by decade. The second chart contains a chilling reminder of the 1980s, in which 11 major freezes were experienced in Orlando and 7 in Tampa. On a positive note, the 1990s have been mild in comparison to earlier decades.

The third chart illustrates the time of year freezes are most likely to occur in Orlando. This suggests that a good time to have a greenhouse ready would be mid-November. The middle of March is a good time to start spring planting. This time frame also applies to southern Florida (although at a much lower risk). For example, a temperature of 32° F was recorded at the Miami airport on March 3, 1980.

**Number of days at 32°F or below**

| Decade | Miami | W. Palm | Tampa | Orlando |
|--------|-------|---------|-------|---------|
| 1950s | 0 | 2 | 15 | 32 |
| 1960s | 0 | 4 | 31 | 24 |
| 1970s | 1 | 6 | 46 | 34 |
| 1980s | 5 | 12 | 32 | 36 |
| 1990-97 | 0 | 0 | 4 | 7 |

**Number of days at 25°F or below**

| Decade | Miami | W. Palm | Tampa | Orlando |
|--------|-------|---------|-------|---------|
| 1950s | 0 | 2 | 1 | 1 |
| 1960s | 0 | 0 | 2 | 2 |
| 1970s | 0 | 0 | 3 | 3 |
| 1980s | 0 | 0 | 7 | 11 |
| 1990-97 | 0 | 0 | 1 | 0 |

**Days with Temperature under 32°F (Orlando, FL.)**

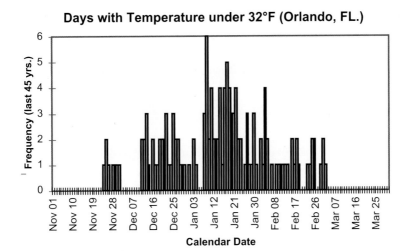

# Hardiness Zones

Approximate range of Average
Annual MINIMUM Temperatures

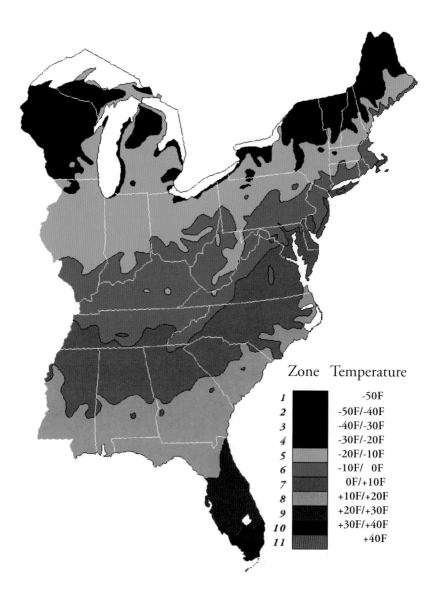

| Zone | Temperature |
|------|-------------|
| 1 | -50F |
| 2 | -50F/-40F |
| 3 | -40F/-30F |
| 4 | -30F/-20F |
| 5 | -20F/-10F |
| 6 | -10F/ 0F |
| 7 | 0F/+10F |
| 8 | +10F/+20F |
| 9 | +20F/+30F |
| 10 | +30F/+40F |
| 11 | +40F |

# Glossary

**Anther** a pollen-containing appendage.

**Bipinnate** a leaf that is divided twice in a pinnate or featherlike pattern.

**Calyx** a cuplike structure that surrounds the base of the flower.

**Corolla** the inner portion of the flower that protrudes from the calyx and surrounds the stamens.

**Cultivar** a variety that originated under cultivation.

**Inflorescence** the arrangement of the flowers on a plant.

**Lanceolate** lance-shaped and tapering towards the end.

**Oblong** rounded at both ends with parallel sides.

**Obovate** similar to oblong leaf shape except larger at the outer end.

**Palmate** having leaflets or lobes of a leaf radiate from a common point.

**Panicle** branched flower clusters loosely arranged on a stem, often pyramidal in shape.

**Pinnate** a leaf in which the leaflets are symmetrically divided along the leaf axis.

**Pistil** the female organ of the flower consisting of ovary, style, and stigma.

**Raceme** a long, unbranched flower spike in which the flowers are borne on individual stems.

**Serrate** having a sawtooth pattern along the edge of a leaf.

**Stamen** the male organ of a flower which contains the pollen-bearing anther and filament.

**Stigma** portion of the pistil (usually at the end of the style) that can receive pollen.

**Style** the long, narrow portion of the pistil with the stigma at the tip and the ovary below.

**Trifoliate** having three leaflets per leaf.

**Umbel** a flower arrangement in which the flower stems originate from a central point.

# Bibliography

Alcoa Steamship Co, Inc. *Flowering Trees of the Caribbean.* New York: Rinehart & Company, Inc., 1951.

Bar-Zvi, David. *Tropical Gardening.* New York: Pantheon Books, 1996.

Constantine, Albert Jr. *Know Your Woods.* New York: Macmillan Co., 1987.

Courtright, Gordon. *Tropicals.* Portland, Oregon: Timber Press, 1988.

Eggenberger, Mary, and Richard Eggenberger. *The Handbook on Oleanders.* Cleveland, Georgia: Tropical Plant Specialists, 1996.

Ellison, Don. *Cultivated Plants of the World.* Brisbane, Australia: Flora Publications International, 1995.

Gentry, A. H. *Bignoniaceae*, monograph no. 25. Bronx, New York: New York Botanical Garden, 1992.

Keay, R. W. J. *Trees of Nigeria.* England: Oxford Science Publications, 1989.

Kelly, H. A. "Pronouncing Latin Words in English," *Classical World,* Vol. 80, Nos. 33 37, 1986.

L. H. Bailey Hortorium. *Hortus Third.* New York: Macmillan Co., 1976.

Macoboy, Stirling. *What Tree is That?* Sydney, Australia: Lansdowne Publishing Pty. Ltd., 1994.

Menninger, Edwin A. *Flowering Trees of the World.* New York: Hearthside Press, Inc., 1962.

Menninger, Edwin A. *Color in the Sky.* Stuart, Florida: Horticultural Books, Inc., 1975.

National Garden Association. *Dictionary of Horticulture.* New York: Macmillan Co., 1987.

Stresau, Frederic B. *Florida, My Eden.* Port Salerno, Florida: Florida Classics Library, 1986.

Sunset Books and Sunset Magazine, ed.: *Trees & Shrubs.* Menlo Park, California: Sunset Publishing Corporation, 1993.

Turner and Wasson: *Botanica.* Milsons Point, New South Wales, Australia: Mynah (imprint of Random House), 1997.

# Index